STEAM POWER Workbooks

GAIL GIBBONS'

FROM SEED TO PLANT
WORKBOOK

HOLIDAY HOUSE · NEW YORK

Dear Parents and Teachers,

We are delighted to share the outstanding work of nonfiction author Gail Gibbons with you, and with the children in your care. This workbook is based on Gibbons' popular *From Seed to Plant,* which teaches children in grades K–1 the fundamentals of the plant life cycle.

Inside this workbook, you will find activities that reinforce not just basic science concepts, but also skills learned in grades K–1. Kids can enjoy activities such as identifying the parts of a flower, learning to write the parts of a plant, circling items that come from plants, and completing mazes that follow a seed's journey. Our book also features a simple project where a child can grow their own bean plant. All the activities in this workbook have been approved by early primary education experts and reinforce the skills being taught at these grade levels.

We hope you agree with us that Gail Gibbons is a master of explaining how the world works to young readers and listeners, and we hope you and the children in your life enjoy this workbook. Please visit our Gail Gibbons website at GailGibbonsbooks.com. We'd love to hear how you are using this book, so let us know at info@holidayhouse.com.

Thank you,

The Editors at Holiday House Books

Contents

The publisher wishes to thank educators Terri Bard
and Myra Zarnowski for reviewing this workbook.

Gail Gibbons' From Seed to Plant Workbook copyright © 2022 by Holiday House Publishing, Inc.

Text and illustrations from *From Seed to Plant* copyright © 1991 by Gail Gibbons
Spot art from *How a House is Built, The Reasons for Seasons, The Art Box, Apples, The Berry Book, Weather Words
and What They Mean, It's Raining, Ice Cream, The Vegetables We Eat, Corn, Hurricanes, Transportation,* and *Flowers*
copyright © 1990, 1995, 1998, 2000, 2002, 2006, 2007, 2008, 2009, 2014, 2017 and 2018 by Gail Gibbons.

HOLIDAY HOUSE is registered in the U.S. Patent and Trademark Office.
Printed and bound in September 2021 at Toppan Leefung, DongGuan, China.
The artwork was created on watercolor paper with black ink, watercolors, and colored pencil.
www.holidayhouse.com
First Edition
1 3 5 7 9 10 8 6 4 2

ISBN: 978-0-8234-5097-8 (workbook)

PLANTS

Animals and plants are alive. They grow and reproduce. Many things are not alive.

Things that *are* alive

Things that *are not* alive

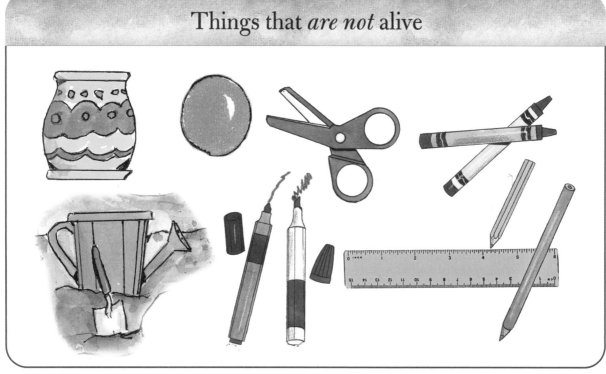

Draw something that *is* alive.

Draw something that *is not* alive.

PLANTS

A plant is different from other living things.
A plant is not an animal. Plants such as grass and trees
are usually rooted in one place.

Animal or plant?
Circle the plants. Make an *X* over the animals.

Trace and write the word *plant*.

plant

Trace and write the word *animal*.

animal

SEEDS

A seed contains the beginnings of a new plant.
Seeds can be different shapes, sizes, and colors.
Trace and write the word *seed*.

seed _____   _____

All seeds grow into the same
kind of plant that made them.

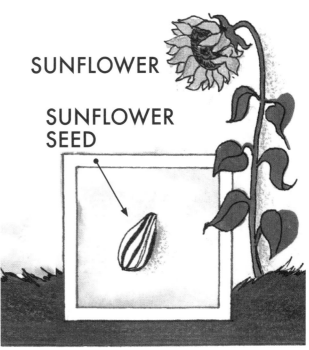

SUNFLOWER

**SUNFLOWER
SEED**

APPLE TREE

APPLE SEEDS

Find the seeds. Circle them.

WATERMELON

PEAS

LEMON

APPLE

SEEDS

Circle the seeds.
Make an *X* over the things that are not seeds.

Draw a circle around the biggest seed.
Some seeds can be eaten as food.
Which seeds can you eat? Mark them with an X.

RASPBERRY

PEACH

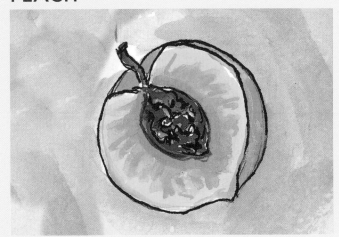

COCONUT

CORN

PEAS

LEMON

SEEDS

The beginning of a plant is curled up inside each seed.
Food is stored inside the seed, too.
The seed has a seed coat to protect it.

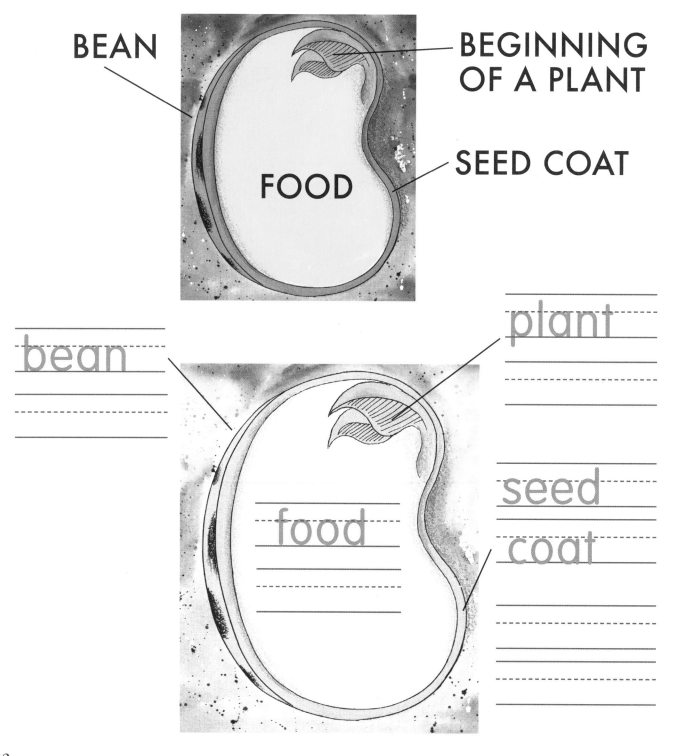

BEAN

BEGINNING OF A PLANT

FOOD

SEED COAT

bean

plant

food

seed coat

Seeds grow inside fruits. Strawberries are the only fruit that has seeds on the outside.

LEMON

STRAWBERRY

WATERMELON

PEACH

CHERRY

PEAR

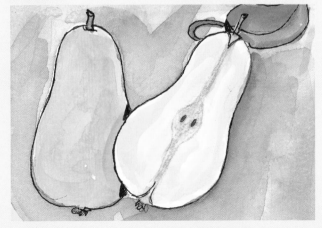

FLOWERS

Many plants grow flowers.
Flowers are where most seeds begin.
Trace the names of the flowers and then write them.

tulip   daisy

rose   violet

buttercup

What other flowers can you name?

PARTS of a FLOWER
A flower is made up of many parts.

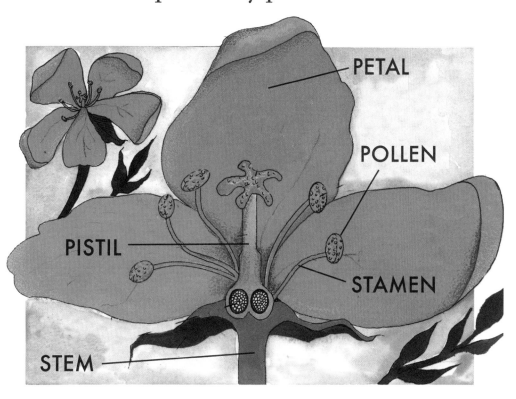

PETAL

POLLEN

PISTIL

STAMEN

STEM

Practice tracing the parts.

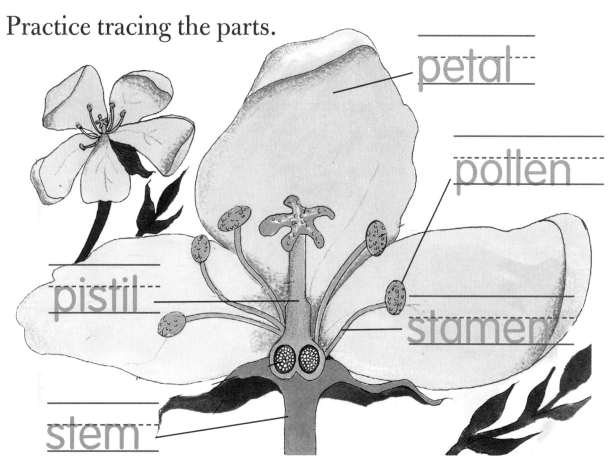

petal

pollen

pistil

stamen

stem

POLLINATION

Pollination happens in different ways. Often, wind blows pollen from flower to flower. Other times, birds or bees take pollen from one flower to another.

POLLEN

POLLEN

POLLEN

Help the hummingbird carry the pollen
from one flower to another.

POLLINATION

When a grain of pollen from a flower lands on a pistil from the same kind of flower, it grows a long tube through the pistil into an ovule. This is the beginning of a seed.

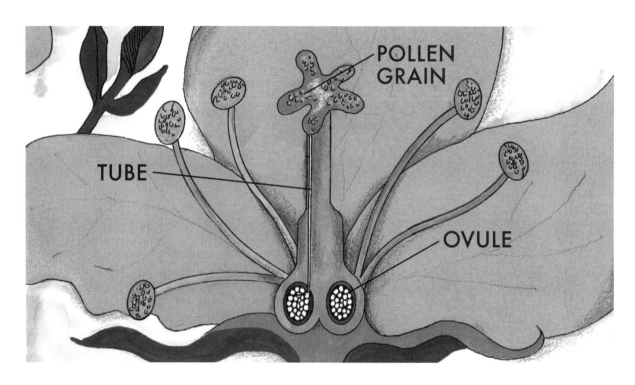

POLLEN GRAIN

TUBE

OVULE

Trace and write the words.

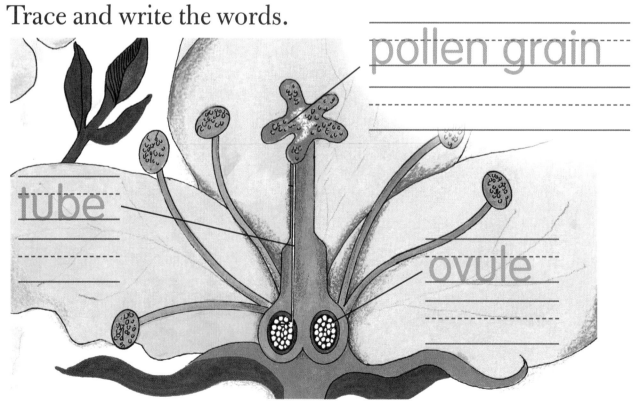

pollen grain

tube

ovule

18

1. The seeds grow inside the flower, even as the flower begins to die.

2. As the seeds become bigger, a fruit or pod grows around them.

3. The fruit or pod protects the seeds.

NIGHTTIME POLLINATION

Some flowers bloom at night.
During the night, they are pollinated.
If plants do not get pollinated, they do not grow
fruits or seeds.

Bees are very important pollinators.
Many farmers need bees to pollinate their crops.
Trace the word and match it to the picture.
Then write the word.

bee

flower

pollen

bird

pistil

SOME SEEDS TRAVEL

The wind scatters seeds. Some seeds have fluff on them that lets them float to the ground like tiny parachutes. Others have wings that spin as they fall.

Many seeds will land somewhere where they can grow, or people may plant seeds.

Help the bird bring the flower seed
to a different place.

SEED NEEDS

Seeds need soil, sun, and water to grow. Practice tracing and writing the words for things that help seeds grow.

SOIL

SUN

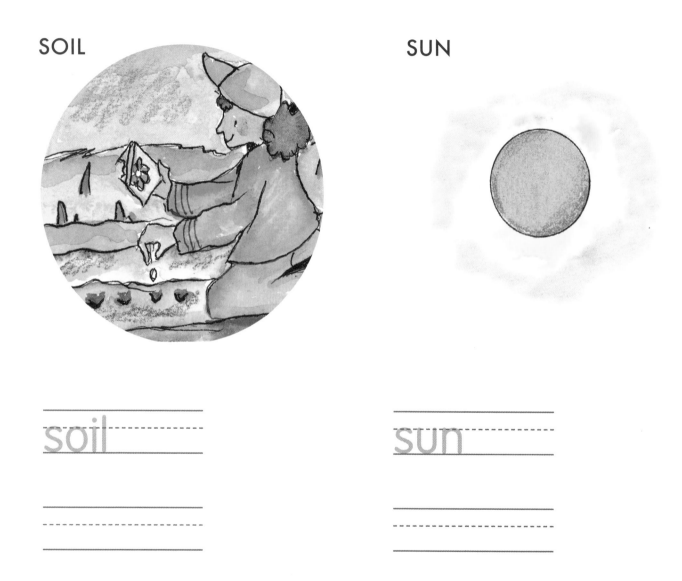

soil

sun

WATER

water

PARTS of a PLANT

Here are the parts of a plant.
Trace the words that show the parts of the plant.
Draw a line to each part.

flower

leaves

stem

roots

Write the parts of a plant.

LEAVES

What do leaves do?
Leaves make food for plants from the water and minerals in the soil, the sunlight, and the air all around the plant.

Here are some leaves. What leaves can you draw in the boxes below?

LILY LEAVES   DAISY LEAVES   CORN LEAVES   APPLE LEAVES

ROOTS

What do roots do?

They collect water and minerals for the plant. They help the plant stay in the ground. Some roots store food for the plant. Many of our vegetables are roots that we eat.

Trace and write the word *root*.

root

Circle the roots.

Three kinds of roots that we eat are turnips, carrots, and radishes. Draw a line from the name of the root vegetable to its picture.

RADISH   **CARROT**   **TURNIP**

  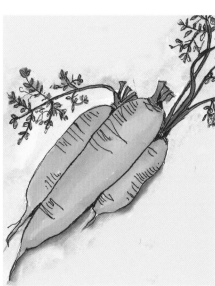

STEMS

What do stems do? The stem holds up the leaves
and flowers. It also sends water and minerals
from the roots to the leaves.
Stems also store nutrients.

Trace and write the word *stem*.

stem

Circle the stems below.

FLOWERS

What do flowers do?

Flowers produce the plant's fruits and seeds.

Plants need flowers to reproduce.

Trace and write the word *flower*.

flower

The petals fall off the flower, and a fruit or pod grows around the seeds. The fruits we eat grow from flowers.

Trace and write the words *flower*, *pod*, and *fruit*.

flower

pod

fruit

THE PLANT LIFE CYCLE

SEED

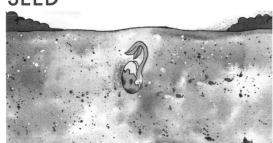

When the sun shines and warms the wet, soft ground, the seed coat breaks open and the seed begins to grow.

ROOT

A root grows down into the soil. The root takes in water and minerals from the soil for food.

LEAVES

Up grows a shoot. Green leaves grow up from the shoot toward the sun. The plant grows bigger. The leaves make food for the plant.

BUDDING and BLOOMING

Finally, the plant is full-grown. Buds on the plant open into flowers where new seeds will grow.

Here is a corn plant.
Can you number its growth stages from 1–4?

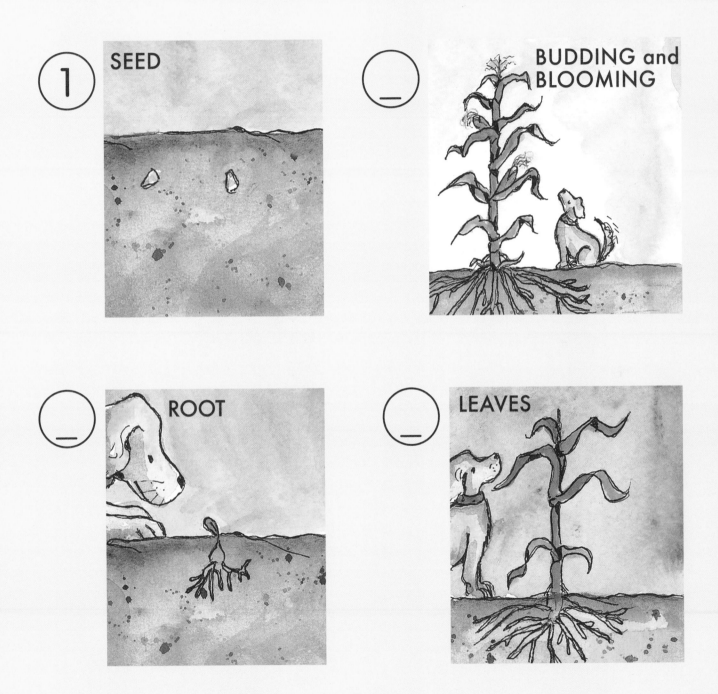

① SEED

◯ BUDDING and BLOOMING

◯ ROOT

◯ LEAVES

GROW YOUR OWN BEAN PLANT

Follow the steps below to grow your own bean plant.

1. Find a clean glass jar. Take a piece of black construction paper and roll it up.

2. Slide the paper into the jar. Fill the jar with water.

3. Wedge the bean seeds between the black paper and the glass. Put the jar in a warm place.

4. In a few days, the seeds will sprout. Watch the roots grow down. The shoots will grow up.

Watch your bean sprouts as they grow!

5. Put dirt into a big clay pot.

6. Carefully remove the small plants from the glass jar. Place them in the soil, covering them up to the base of their shoots.

Water them . . . and watch them grow!

Draw pictures of your beans as they grow.

My beans in a jar

My seeds beginning to sprout

My plants in a pot

My plants beginning to grow

We need plants so we can eat them!
Each one of these foods you eat is a part of a plant.
Draw a line from the picture to the word that tells
what it is.

FRUIT   STEM   LEAF

SEED   ROOT

We need plants for many things, including food, clothing, buildings, and medicine.
Which things come from plants? Circle them.

Scissors

Salad dressing

Jams

Plastics

Metal bucket

Wood for building houses

Soaps

Cotton cloth

Medicines

Televisions

Wheat flour, bread, muffins

Markers

FLOUR

Answer Key

Pages 6-7

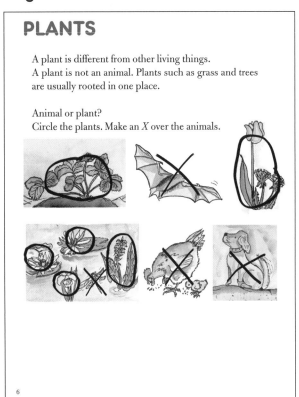

PLANTS

A plant is different from other living things.
A plant is not an animal. Plants such as grass and trees are usually rooted in one place.

Animal or plant?
Circle the plants. Make an *X* over the animals.

Page 9

All seeds grow into the same kind of plant that made them.

APPLE TREE
APPLE SEEDS
SUNFLOWER
SUNFLOWER SEED

Find the seeds. Circle them.

WATERMELON
PEAS
LEMON
APPLE

Pages 10-11

SEEDS

Circle the seeds.
Make an *X* over the things that are not seeds.

Draw a circle around the biggest seed.
Some seeds can be eaten as food.
Which seeds can you eat? Mark them with an *X*.

RASPBERRY   PEACH

COCONUT   CORN

LEMON   PEAS

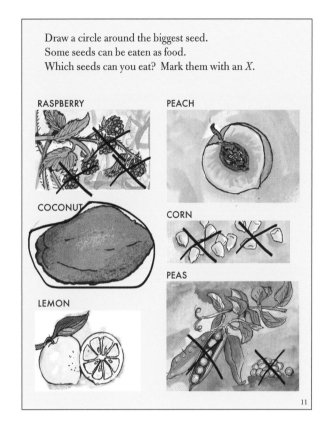

Page 17

Help the hummingbird carry the pollen from one flower to another.

17

Page 23

Help the bird bring the flower seed to a different place.

Page 27

Write the parts of a plant.

flower

leaves

stem

roots

27

ROOTS

What do roots do?
They collect water and minerals for the plant. They help the plant stay in the ground. Some roots store food for the plant. Many of our vegetables are roots that we eat.

Circle the roots.

30

Three kinds of roots that we eat are turnips, carrots, and radishes. Draw a line from the name of the root vegetable to its picture.

RADISH   CARROT   TURNIP

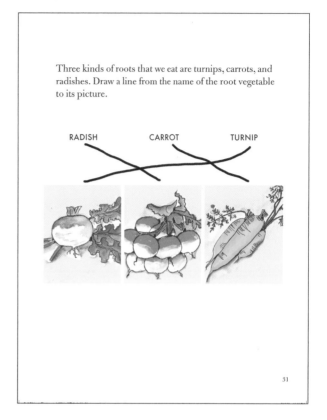

31

Page 33

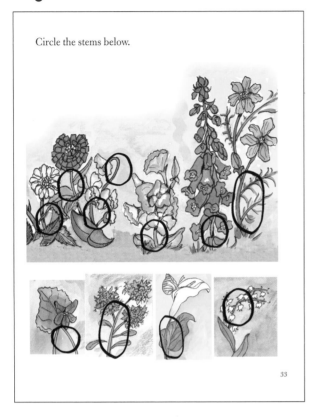

Circle the stems below.

Page 37

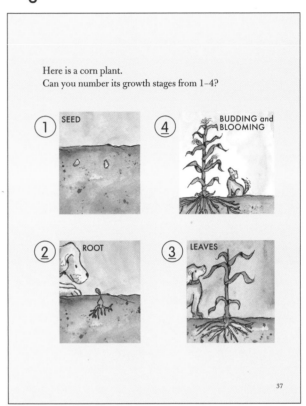

Here is a corn plant.
Can you number its growth stages from 1–4?

1 SEED

4 BUDDING and BLOOMING

2 ROOT

3 LEAVES

Page 40

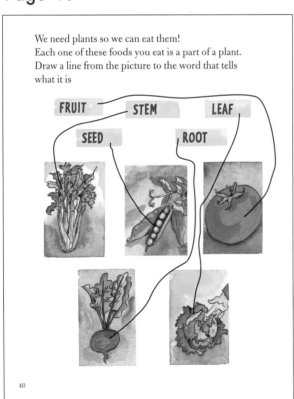

We need plants so we can eat them!
Each one of these foods you eat is a part of a plant.
Draw a line from the picture to the word that tells
what it is

FRUIT   STEM   LEAF

SEED   ROOT

We need plants for many things, including food, clothing, buildings, and medicine.
Which things come from plants? Circle them.

Salad dressing: Salad dressings are often made with vegetable oils.

Jams: Jams are made with fruit.

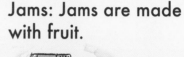

Soaps: Soaps can have vegetable oil and can be scented with flowers.

Cotton cloth: Cotton is a plant that can be made into clothing and fabric.

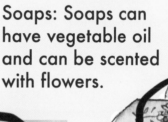

Wood for building houses: Wood comes from trees.

Medicines: Some medicines come from plants.

Wheat flour, bread, muffins: Flour can come from wheat, barley, and other grains.

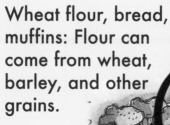

Young Botanist Certificate

Congratulations!

You have learned all about what happens in the journey from seed to plant. You have learned about the parts of a seed and the parts of a plant and what plants are used for.

You are now a young botanist, a student in the study of plants.

_____
Name

_____
Date

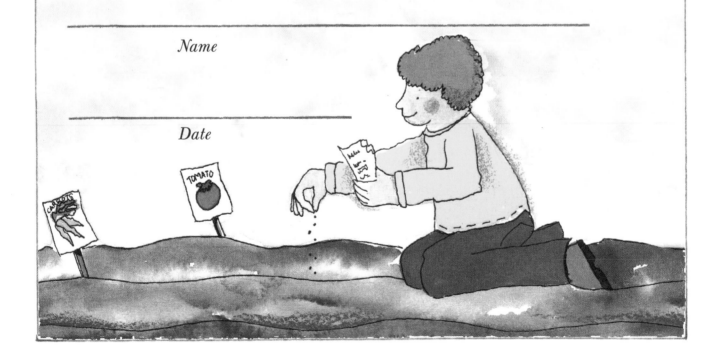